A Kid's Guide to
Keeping Family First

Written by
J.S. Jackson

Illustrated by
R. W. Alley

ONE
CARING
PLACE

Abbey Press
St. Meinrad, IN 47577

This one is for my younger sister, Sally—
my one and only sibling—
who went through childhood with me
and was by far the brightest light
in our strange and wonderful family.
I am eternally grateful for her love,
her support and her limitless generosity
in lending money for the purchase
of musical instruments for the band.

Text © 2005 J.S. Jackson
Illustrations © 2005 St. Meinrad Archabbey
Published by One Caring Place
Abbey Press
St. Meinrad, Indiana 47577

Library of Congress Catalog Number
2004097519

ISBN 0-87029-390-7

Printed in the United States of America

A Message to Parents, Teachers, and Other Caring Adults

The beginning of this century has proved to be one of the most challenging times in human history. Communications of all kinds race around the planet at lightning speed, bombarding us with sensational and frightening stories many times a day. Now more than ever, the hope for our children and their future lies within the strength and the promise of the family.

The family can be a safe haven, a confidence-maker, a character-builder, a self-esteem enhancer. It can teach love and kindness, honesty, and generosity. By far, the most important building blocks children need to achieve successful, happy lives rise from the foundations of a healthy, secure family.

Families need to work at keeping communication lines open with their children at all ages and all stages. While most parents understand the need for *parent-to-child* communication—this most basic human instinct to pass on our knowledge, our love, our values, and our heritage to our children—it is also necessary to understand the need for *child-to-parent* communication. Children need to be listened to and empathized with.

Family rituals, such as morning and/or nightly mealtimes, are indispensable in establishing a strong, happy family. Morning meals allow family members to start the day on a "high note." Evening meals offer the opportunity for concentrated communication, sharing of feelings, fun, and laughter. Other rituals, like regular attendance at religious services, as well as family activities like picnics or miniature golf, are equally important to the strength and cohesiveness of a family.

"Keeping family first" is a simple concept, but one that can easily be lost in all the options and attractions our daily lives present to us. It asks that every family member be prepared to make small sacrifices for the overall good of the family.

The easiest thing about keeping *your* family first is that it takes only two things: you and your child. Reading this book together should give you plenty of ideas of how to make that happen.

—*J.S. Jackson*

What Is a Family?

A family is a group of people who love each other and live together.

Many families have a mom and dad, some kids, and maybe some pets. Other families have just one parent and one or more kids. Some families have grandparents or other relatives living with them.

Some families are "blended." This happens when a mom from one family marries a dad from another family to make a brand new family.

A Strong Family

In a strong family, both the adults and the children help each other. They are loving, kind, giving, and honest with one another.

Parents are like teachers, showing their children how to do things—like riding a bike, or making a cake, or cleaning up their rooms. Parents also try to teach their kids "values"—how to be polite, get along with others, and become a loving person.

Children teach their parents too. They show their mom and dad what it's like to be a kid, how they feel, and what they need.

Family Talk

It's very important for families to talk and listen to each other. Talk with your parents every day and let them know what's going on in your life. Tell them what you're feeling— the good stuff *and* the bad stuff.

Can you think of ways to tell your parents something *without* talking? You can tell your dad you love him by giving him a hug. Or by doing a chore without being asked. Or by keeping your room looking nice.

Family Traditions

"Traditions" are things that you do over and over, which mean a lot to you. Your family probably has certain ways of celebrating holidays—special decorations, foods, parties, and gifts. These are your family traditions.

If your family background is Irish, Mexican, Italian, or Polish, for example, you may have traditions from these countries.

Traditions don't have to be about holidays. Any special family event—a picnic in the park, going to the movies, a vacation at the lake—can become a family tradition.

The Family Meal

One of the most important family traditions happens every day—the evening meal. This is a great chance for everybody to be together and talk about how their day went.

It's always nice to take a moment to pray before eating, to thank God for giving you this food and your family to share it with. Some families like to join hands while doing this.

Mealtime is a good time for all to share how the day went, what they did, and how they feel about it. You can talk about things you're happy and proud about, or things that made you feel bad.

Sharing Your Faith

Many families have a weekly tradition of going to church or some other place to pray. There's an old saying: "Families that pray together stay together." Your family's faith is a strong tie that you share and can call upon when times get tough.

Making weekly trips to a place of prayer is a great family tradition. You can learn about God and how to pray. You can feel a part of the "faith family" as you listen to the readings, sing songs, and pray together.

Family Meetings

Many families plan weekly family meetings to catch up with each other and settle any problems.

Some families use a "talking stick," as Native Americans used to call it. Only the person holding the stick may talk. When *you* are holding the stick, everyone in the family has to listen to you. The stick is passed from person to person until everyone has said what they need to say.

It doesn't even have to be a stick. You could have a "talking spoon" if you want, or even a "talking spatula"! But this is a good way to make sure everyone gets a chance to talk and be heard.

When Kids Fight

When any people live together, fighting is bound to happen. It's okay to get mad, but try to "fight fair." Fair fighting means *telling* the other person how you feel—without hitting, hurting, or saying anything mean.

You could say to your sister, "I'm really upset because you played my new game without asking me, and now some of the pieces are lost." Always try to start with the word "I." "I feel bad when you…" or "I don't like it when you…."

Listen to what the other person has to say, too. Then try to work out a plan that makes both of you happy.

When Parents Fight

Almost all parents fight at one time or another. And almost all kids think it's scary. Parents are big and their voices are louder.

It's best to leave them alone and let them work it out. Many parents feel closer after they let off steam and then make up.

Just remember that people who love each other can still get angry with each other. It's like a cloud passing in front of the sun. For a little while the sunshine is gone, but you know it's still there, and it always returns.

Working Together

It takes a lot of time and work to keep a family and home going. Parents need kids to help as much as they can.

You may have chores that you do every day, like feeding the dog or setting the table. Try to remember to do them without your mom or dad having to nag you.

A big family job—like doing yard work or cleaning out the garage—can be fun when you do it together. You'll feel proud when it's finished, and then everyone will have more time for fun!

Playing Together

Kids often have many sports and other things going on. Be sure to make some free time with your family just to play together.

If the weather is good, you could go to a park with a picnic basket and a Frisbee, or swim in a lake or pool. If the weather is bad, you might want to go to a museum or aquarium.

In the winter, some families play "Lights Out." You pretend that the electricity has gone off. All you have are candles, books, cards, board games, and each other. (No TV, radio, computer, or video games.) You will be amazed at how much fun you'll have!

Your Bigger Family

Most people have what are called "extended families." These are made up of your grandmothers and grandfathers, cousins, aunts, and uncles.

If you are lucky, some of these people will live nearby, so you can get together often for family events. If they don't live nearby, you may still be able to get together for holidays or vacations.

When you are together with your relatives, ask them about your family history and stories. These are the things that make families *families*.

Keeping Family First

Families are usually very busy. They have work, school, homework, sports, lessons, friends, and meetings. It takes extra-special effort to keep family first.

Family time is so important, though, that sometimes parents or kids may have to give up something else to spend time together. This might mean putting off a sleepover or not going to a movie with friends. For a parent, it might mean skipping an exercise class or golf game.

There is nothing more caring or loving than giving up something you really want to do— to be with your family.

There's No Place Like Family

In the movie *The Wizard of Oz*, Dorothy keeps saying, "There's no place like home, there's no place like home." And she's right, there IS no place like home. Because home is where your family is.

No one will ever know you like your family. No one will ever accept you like your family. No one will ever love you like your family.

Family is one of God's most wonderful blessings, and it needs our special loving care.

J. S. Jackson is a husband, dad, and writer living in Lenexa, Kansas. The former manager of Hallmark Cards' creative writing staff, he is now a freelance writer and editor. A multi-tasking "Mr. Mom," he creates cards, books, and other inspirational materials from his messy home office. He is presently in the process of writing a book called *Safe at Home*, about how important it is for kids to feel safe in their home environment.

R. W. Alley is the illustrator for the popular Abbey Press adult series of Elf-help books, as well as an illustrator and writer of children's books. He lives in Barrington, Rhode Island, with his wife, daughter, and son.